WEST IRONBOUND

Portrait of an Island

WEST IRONBOUND

Portrait of an Island

Published by Foggy Cove Books
P.O. Box 84
Riverport, Nova Scotia, B0J 2W0
Canada

Printed and bound in Canada by Friesens, Altona, Manitoba.

Canadian Cataloguing in Publication Data available upon request.

Softcover ISBN: 978-0-9877086-0-1 $29.95
Hardcover ISBN: 978-0-9877086-0-8

First printing August 2011

The publication of the first edition coincided with an exhibition of images from the book,
held in August 2011 at anderson, gallery of contemporary photography in Lunenburg, Nova Scotia
(andersonmontague.com).

A portion of the proceeds from the sale of this book will support the Kingsburg Coastal Conservancy's
fundraising campaign to acquire West Ironbound Island.

Mariëtte Roodenburg | *Photographs*

Christine Higdon | *Design*

Larry Gaudet | *Words*

We are grateful to the following people who so generously
stepped forward to protect West Ironbound.

PATRONS

Alex MacDonald & Michael Arnoldi
Anne C. Baker
Moira Ruskell & Arthur Billard
Alan & Chris Bromstein
Robert Drolet & Marian R. Cameron
Annette & John Campbell
Iris & Dave Cosh
Avy Dolgoy
Patricia & Stewart Early
Ferrier Kimball Thomas, Lawyers,
    Bridgewater, NS
Scott, Donna & Sarah Fleming
    in memory of Muriel Munroe
Mary Ann & Wayne Fulcher
Noreen Channels & Don Galbraith
Alison Smith & Larry Gaudet
Trish, Ian & John Godfrey
Darrell & Brian Gregersen
Rudy Haase
Marie-Therese O'Neill & John Heelan
Barbara & Andrew Hilburt
Margaret Homans, Marian Homans-Turnbull,
    & Sylvia Homans

William Taylor & Marion Homer
Richard Brown & Deborah Kennedy-Brown
Saskia, Sebastian, Elizabeth & Nikolas Kirby
Susan deWitt & Pierre Lesperance
Elizabeth Wishart & Bruce MacCormack
Inez Uerz & Stephen MacDonald
Carter & Charlie McDowell
Anne & Eric Mills
Mariëtte Roodenburg & Toon Nagtegaal
Robert Buckley & Judith Nelson
Nancy Nicholson
Michael & Cara Peterman
Mrs. Janet Piers
Alicia Crooks & Robert Risley
Maribeth Solomon & Robert Schwartz
Karen & Steve Shapiro
Malcolm Moffat & Louise Smith
Vivian & Stanley Smith
Christine Higdon & Tracy Westell
Kenneth Young, Young & Associates
    Real Estate Appraisals and Consultants

WEST IRONBOUND is a 120-acre island along the Atlantic coast of southern Nova Scotia, near the dune beaches of the Kingsburg peninsula and the mouth of the LaHave River.

In the mid-eighteenth century, the island was settled as a fishing outport. A century later, a local family moved there as lighthouse keepers, and for several generations they also worked a small potato farm and kept sheep. The human community is long gone but sheep still roam the island, the current flock tended by farmers who commute from the mainland.

West Ironbound is a coastal wonderland that includes a thriving rookery for Great Blue Herons and abundant space for other nesting birds.

In 2010, the Kingsburg Coastal Conservancy (KCC), a local land trust and charitable organization, acquired half the island to safeguard it from development and to preserve its ecological integrity. At the same time, in support of the KCC's work, a generous individual who wishes to remain anonymous, purchased the other half of the island.

The publication of this book joins other fundraising activities intended to assist the KCC in buying the second part of West Ironbound so that the island remains protected and accessible forever.

44°13' 60 N

64°16' 60 w

SUMMER

From the dune beach and through the mist, the island across the bay reveals its longest, least vulnerable flank: a serenely jagged scar on the horizon.

The island is all muscled shadow this morning, barnacles of cliff topped by a sawtoothed line of dark trees. The landward prow is a steep slope of cleared green. It also has a black tail, a thorny rudder of shoal, flickering in the spray of crashing waves.

The island nearly touches the headland enclosing the outer bay. Maybe the two were joined in distant geological time, a billion storms ago.

The two coastlines are etched against the sky in tense opposition. Even so, the tranquil sea that keeps them apart suggests a more sympathetic relationship, as if they're already joined underwater: siblings forever, in good times and bad, with secrets only they share.

If the island is not swimming toward land, you're ready to believe it's lurking with intent, protecting the bay and the sandy shoreline crescent. Perhaps it's stalking something? You think it's only a kilometre away but it's more like three.

Even in its vast stillness, the island convinces you that it's on the move.

That it has a plan – a mission – a destiny – involving you.

The illusion of forceful proximity – of intimate connection – it's there.

It looks like a whale – a beast from the depths –

Or a warrior ship from another planet or another time –

What's there – what's reaching you – is more elusive and disorienting. It's an island but its physical character disappears the harder and longer you look.

Soon after the small fishing boat leaves the harbour, you realize it wasn't built for unruly seas and bad weather. The gunwales are barely wide enough to sit on.

Everything below creaks and strains.

The diesel roar and diesel fumes.

In the flat noon light, the water looks oily blue.

Approaching the open sea past the river mouth, the wind strengthens while the cliffs along the coast diminish. The boat ploughs ahead, fighting each wave head on.

One wave eludes the bow, slams into starboard.

The spray ignites the light in the air around you.

The closer you get, the more vertical and dimensional the meadow and trees and cliffs become. The island rises up to greet you, as daunting as a cathedral, or the mouth of a gentle monster at rest.

The engines cut, the boat ebbs forward until it recoils along the anchor line.

A protected cove fronted by a small beach draped in seaweed.

The feeling of being welcomed spreads through you.

You've dreamed of this moment for years.

Soon you're in the shallow water yourself, pulling the dory up onto the beach.

You pause to orient yourself, the water dripping from your legs.

Barely a ripple in the bay. The lapping of incoming tide.

A warm breeze whispers toward you through the long grass.

The birds complain.

The air smells good enough to eat.

The land feels unusually solid, your balance a little shaky after an hour at sea.

You gaze into everything –

The green meadow rolls away and forever, unravelling into limitless blue.

In the sun, the green house also rises, a gable pointing skyward into blue.

So much colour sculpting every first impression.

Your eye can only submit, and travel where directed, thoughtlessly.

People willingly settled on the island, and routinely used very small boats to ferry oxen and sheep over. What blend of necessity and choice brought them here?

You could easily pose the same unanswerable question to yourself.

It's sheep-shearing time.

The fence is unfolded and erected in the field, a string of posts and wire to contain the sheep, extending from the holding pen down to the water.

The group fans out in search of the flock. The first sighting is on the other side of a spruce thicket: a woolly mass with downturned heads among many more legs.

The sheep disappear – silently. Spooked by a cough.

They emerge again into a sliver of peripheral vision. Then disappear again.

Hide-and-go-seek. This goes on for an hour or so.

The shouting and arm-waving begins –

Laughter – everyone holding hands –

The panicked sheep rush into the field, away from the herders.

The human chain moves them into the holding pen.

The work of the island never ends –

You study the sky as if you've never seen a sunset before, as if you're the first person in the history of civilization to stand apart in wonder.

The moment teases you into thinking it'll go on forever. That it's worth standing there trying to distinguish precisely where and when the orange becomes pink then rose then something darker, all those blues that will soon blacken.

Stare for as long and unblinking as you like.

To experience the change – the shift – first you need to look away –

Return to what you were doing – talk to someone – think of something –

Then look back again –

Now marvel at what has happened in your absence.

The last shorn sheep is released into the dark.

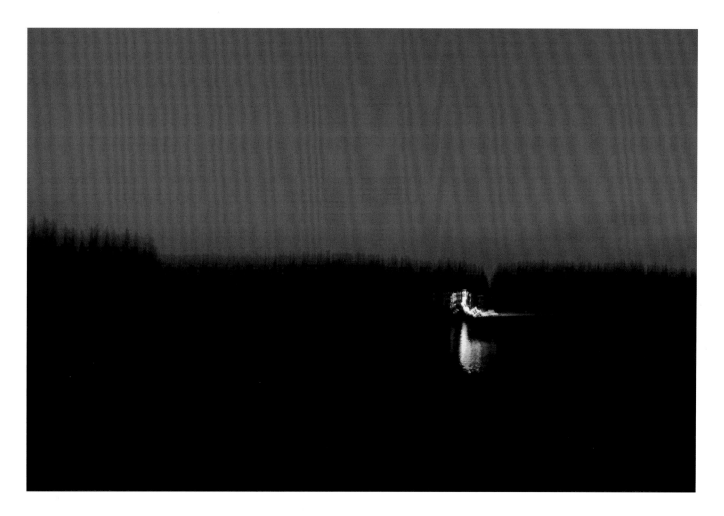

FALL

You fall in behind the others.

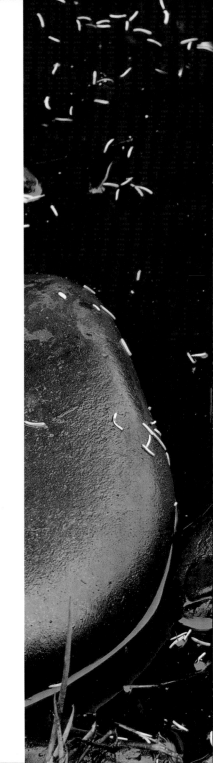

The search starts in the field, moving east along the beach toward higher ground. Soon you're around the bend into the eastern exposure, the barren cliffs that rear back from the sea, the ravaged gullies of slate bedrock.

The ground cover is stunted greenery and browned lichen over stone, a flimsy carpet of what can cling and never rise, weighed down by uncountable shards of flat rock.

Here and there a deformed tree emerges from a crevice.

And there they are.

Most are crouching. All mute.

An ear flickers from time to time, the only movement you can detect.

You turn away for an instant and when you turn back, they're gone.

The wind bites and stings.

The scents harden. More metal, iron, salt.

Ferns withered to a crisp.

You can't understand a storm by tracking it on a screen in the palm of your hand –

Telling you when it's ending and why –

You need to be in the sound and fury of it –

How else would you really know when it passes?

Orange and red and brown leaves floating in puddles of marsh.

It's possible here in this season to witness the miracle of endless life outlasting the spectacle of cyclical – or temporary – death.

Nothing dies forever here.

What does die – what dies everywhere – is –

However you define it –

Consciousness – memory – spirit – the expression of experience within the living form – something definitely dies while becoming something else.

Who has the courage to accept life as ashes emptied from an urn into the wind?

If living forever meant the death of love – would you still want to live?

Autumn is a postcard with a sadder story to tell.

Counter-clockwise you go around the island, continuing the search for sheep.

You go back in time –

From the mid-eighteenth century people lived here for generations and then they didn't and now they live again in sepia images and oral histories archived in church basements and on websites run by local heritage groups.

Those who lived here would have fused into a coalition of dependency and strangeness. The bonds were tight, the silences long and expressive, the grudges longer and managed at times through varied forms of emotional shunning.

What was love – or passion – in this world? Happiness? Anger? Sanity?

Self-sufficiency was everything here.

What they didn't bring here, they made. Or grew.

What they took back, they traded or sold.

Compare their lives to yours –

In every tree, you see the scenic possibility, a painting, an evergreen accent in the brown fields and grey sky. They would have seen oars, fences, joists, firewood.

In the air, you see an alluring composition of dynamic elements. They would have seen weather, anticipating a change, days in advance.

They would have seen the coming of winter – and prepared.

You feel connected to them in only fundamental ways.

You wonder where – or if – they buried their dead here.

The clouds are towering phantoms.

The island seems the loneliest place today, submissive to the turbulence it endures with infinite stability.

Along the northern coast you can see the mainland and the village you left behind. It all looks so small, provisional. As if it could disappear tomorrow.

It feels strange to look back at your world like this.

It's like you've never been there before.

They can't hide forever.

The sheep finally do as sheep do: accept confinement.

It's now time to take all the male sheep back to the mainland and then to the butcher.

One by one, the males are carried from the holding pen to the dory in confused agitation, then rowed out and loaded into the fishing boat.

The females remain behind –

WINTER

Rugged terrain, up and down, the way forward blocked from time to time by fallen trees. Too often you end up on ledges, on terraces of granite, dusted in ice.

The crunching of your boots –

You break through thin crusts of white into soft powdered white.

The snow muffles every other sound. You've never felt more inside yourself.

The warmth of the winter day, the melting snow, the bright blue of the sea –

All give way now to cold and darkness.

This trip was timed to bring the ram back as late in the year as possible.

This will ensure that no lambs are born too early, in deep winter, when their chances of survival would be much lower.

Where has the time gone?

It's a small island, and impossible to get lost, but you've been walking in circles longer than you'd like to admit.

You descend into a ravine open to the sea, bottomed in pebbles and driftwood at low tide. You walk slowly across it, breaking into thin ice between the stones, careful not to slip on the sea grass. How would you get across at high tide?

The sea is quiet except for the echo of waves crashing somewhere else.

About a hundred years ago, a steamer was marooned on a shoal near here in a winter storm. When the weather cleared, a cable was strung from the ship's mast to a tree onshore. Women and children were strapped, one at a time, into a wicker ballast basket and hauled to safety on the island. The men were ferried ashore in dories provided by local schooners that joined the rescue effort.

You're heading south, toward the middle of the island and the high pasture that leads back to the cove, and the house.

From within the forested darkness, an opening.

You're back on the scavenged eastern plateau where the automated beacon is bolted to steel scaffolding. Its concrete base is impressively spotted in bird shit.

The lighthouse itself has been gone for decades.

You contemplate the horizon the way it has always looked from here. Only a passing ship could temporarily humanize the perspective.

There really should be an old-fashioned lighthouse here.

The site feels like an ancient ruin, missing its temple, worthy of an archeological dig. It looks like where you'd come to fall on your knees and speak to your god.

Where you'd pass judgment – or not.

Where you'd confront the part of yourself no one else has ever seen.

Where you actually do contemplate how fortunate you are.

Snow falling through the windless night –

SPRING

In the sunshine and strong winds –

You inch along splintered slate under attack from waves that cascade and fizzle toward you then recede in a clatter.

The tide is relentless in a way that makes you aware of the planetary spin. You close your eyes. You try to breathe in time with the rhythm.

You'd like to believe the island beneath you is doing the same: that within its massiveness there are lungs or gills or something that breathes – and lives – like you do, subject to the same forces and mysteries.

You came out today to see how many lambs were born over the winter.

Enough to make everyone smile.

In this minute there is time for a hundred reflections –

You belong here, or some part of you does. If not your body, then your gaze: what you project at the island from a distance – from wherever you are.

Or you don't belong here – not yet.

After all, the magical island is only truly approachable after all the trials of character have been endured and the truth revealed about who you are.

If that were only so –

You want the island to be alive – that's the heart of it.

And why that is – you don't know why – but if you can believe the island lives in the way that you live – if you can believe it breathes as you breathe – if you can for an unreal minute believe all that and more – then maybe there's a possibility of a conversation, a way to see your relationship as a friendship.

You want to speak to it on your terms – on whatever terms are available.

You want the island to teach you something. What? It doesn't matter what.

What the island wants is another story.

It's not an image or an idea that will ever be captured with certainty.

The island is the geography of a journey that goes in many directions at once as you experience it. It's the walk you take inside and beyond yourself every day, usually without noticing. It's as much a part of you as anything else.

From here, you know your way home.

Acknowledgements

MARIËTTE ROODENBURG

West Ironbound Island is a beautiful place; many fall for its magic and develop a special connection to the island. Some of those I need to thank in particular, because this book would not have been this book without them.

Thank you: John Campbell for asking me to make photographs of the island for the Kingsburg Coastal Conservancy – that really got things going.

Thank you: Jake Wentzel, for taking me along on several sheep round-ups – all I know about sheep, except how they taste, I learned from you.

Thank you: Gerald Mossman, for taking me around the island in "Olde Moss" in Arctic circumstances and for trying so hard to get me on to the island throughout the winter – it certainly was a freak winter.

Thank you: Inez Uerz, for generously sharing your knowledge and experience as a professional fund raiser with us.

Thank you Larry and Christine for embracing this project with passion and for giving it all your creative genius – it has been such a joy working with you.

Above all, I need to thank my husband, Toon Nagtegaal, for his unwavering support. Thank you, Antonio, for yet another wonderful adventure together.

LARRY GAUDET

Thank you: Stan and Vivian Smith for love and support over many years. Stan is the unsung hero of this project for me. Toon Nagtegaal for his brainpower and exceptional contributions throughout this project, for the stories about his sister that affected how this book was written, and for support on a previous book. Louise Smith and Malcolm Moffat for their incredible generosity and support. Donna and James. My friends in Kingsburg and everywhere (including my neighbours who volunteer with the KCC). Tracy Westell for seeding creative possibilities. The KCC Board. My collaborators Christine and Mariëtte. And to Mariëtte and Toon yet again for the vision, the stomach and the generosity to undertake this project. To Alison, Jackson and Theo with all my love.

CHRISTINE HIGDON

Many thanks to—The sheep, for more than a century of Nova Scotian endurance. Stan, for being the one who, probably unbeknownst to him, lit my way to this project. Jake the shepherd, for his glorious tour of West Ironbound. The ocean, for calling me from West to East. Tracy and Avy, for bringing me here. All the generous donors. My partners in crime, for inviting me to join them, for the fun, for their intelligence: Mariëtte (exquisite photographs), Larry (beautiful words), and Toon (inspirational herding of cats). And to my most wonderful cowboys, large and small—Paddy, Ben, and Trace—with love.

KINGSBURG COASTAL CONSERVANCY

6 June 2011

Dear Friends of West Ironbound Island and Nova Scotia's Seacoast,

The preservation of West Ironbound Island as a uniquely precious natural resource for the Kingsburg peninsula, the LaHave River basin and Nova Scotia is at the heart of the mission of the Kingsburg Coastal Conservancy.

Put simply, our guiding objective is to protect our special part of Nova Scotia's south shore and its natural beauty for the public. Thus, the KCC is thrilled to partner with Kingsburg residents Mariëtte Roodenburg, Toon Nagtegaal, Christine Higdon and Larry Gaudet who together produced and published a new book about the island, *West Ironbound, Portrait of an Island.*

It's our hope that the publication of this wondrous book will encourage others who value the appealing nature of our coastal areas to support not only the purchase and, hence, the preservation of West Ironbound Island, but to also actively participate in the protection of Nova Scotia's coastline and numerous islands . . . a potentially all-too-fleeting resource for the people of our province.

Gratefully,

The Board of the Kingsburg Coastal Conservancy

Bob Buckley   John Campbell   Marilyn Congdon

Dave Cosh   Marion Homer   Alex MacDonald

Stan Smith   Rick Welsford

www.kccns.org